AFRICAN AMERICAN NUTRITION

LEARN HOW TO USE NUTRITION TO YOUR ADVANTAGE AND RECLAIM POWER OVER YOUR HEALTH

KATHERINE LAWRENCE

WITH SPECIAL CONTRIBUTIONS BY JACQUELYNE SAMUELS

Cover image © Shutterstock.com

www.innovativeinkpublishing.com
Send all inquiries to:
4050 Westmark Drive
Dubuque, IA 52004-1840

Published in the United States of America

KATHERINE LAWRENCE

Katherine Lawrence is a Cornell and Stanford educated nutritionist who grew up in her grandmother's kitchen in Louisiana. She and her husband Matt own Food Saved Me, a health and wellness resource for the community in Southlake, Texas.

Food Saved Me offers free nutrition classes to the community and also is an authorized Saladmaster cookware dealership.

Katherine reversed her infertility and reproductive disease 18 years ago using diet and healthy cooking techniques, and went on to have three sons. Having taught over 10,000 students she has witnessed countless disease recoveries using the science and practical tips she shares in her classes. Katherine has a deep appreciation for the African-American culture, including its history and delicious food, and prays this class will bless and multiply throughout this community.

JACQUELYNE (JACQUI) SAMUELS

Jacqui has been a Saladmaster owner since October 2016 and joined the Food Saved Team in November 2016. She's now a Premier Platinum Distributor, assisting the office with Team leadership as well as being an avid cooking consultant in her own right. She takes pride in being a people person for all races, kinds and creeds; however, it would be fair to say the Black & African American population make up the largest group she has served. This service has provided a front row seat to the necessity of this class for this culture.

Jacquelyne was born and raised in southeast Texas, with deep family roots from both the southern and southern areas of Louisiana. Cajun and soul foods were weekly cuisines prepared in her home. Her daddy began teaching her how to cook, from scratch, at the young age of 11. Delicious meals filled with an abundance of flavor, executed with seasoning, butter and sugar was her norm!

While her love for food was nurtured at a young age, as an adult, this love turned into a love/hate dichotomy due to the negative affect these things could have on our health.

For this reason, Jacquelyne has contributed to this class in hopes of being a conduit in bridging the differences to similarities.

SPECIAL THANKS

This class is dedicated to the amazing and diverse cooking coaches and customers of Food Saved Me in Southlake, Texas. You have gently educated me and opened my eyes to the struggles of African Americans and inspired me to learn more. I owe a special thanks to Jacquelyne Samuels for providing context, perspective and input for this life-changing class. Her contributions helped make my data-searching personal and certainly enriched my understanding of her culture. Some of the information presented in this class is uncomfortable and controversial. As a nutritionist, after conducting a thorough investigation of the research decided to include all the data and let you draw own conclusions. Take this as a starting point, to conduct your own investigations and decide what best fits for your health.

Part of our mission at Food Saved Me is to bless the community… to make it better. We hope this class and its information propagate throughout the African American community to inspire more awareness, more healthy options and more hope. I celebrate our differences and am grateful to be on this journey with you.

In love and constant pursuit of the truth,

Katherine

TABLE OF CONTENTS

AFRICAN AMERICANS, AS COMPARED TO NON-HISPANIC CAUCASIANS:

-Have the highest death rates from all forms of cancer.

-Have more asthma and are 3 times more likely to die from it.

-Are 3 times more likely to have lung sarcoidosis and 16 times more likely to die from it.

-Have a SIDS (sudden-infant-death-syndrome) 2.5 times higher

-Are 50% more likely to get lung cancer, even though their smoking rates have decreased.

-Have 2 times more diabetes and with more severe complications.

-Have much higher rates of heart disease and stroke, due to very high incidence of high blood pressure.

-At age 20, 42% of African American men & 45% of African American women have high-blood pressure.

-Children are 3 times more likely to have sleep apnea.

-Have a stroke rate of 4 times higher between the ages of 35-54.

(DeNoon, 2017) (CDC, 2017)

"Race, as we think of them, arose as a result of spontaneous mutations...that were beneficial in a particular environment, which survived and were passed on."

- Barbara Dixon. African American cardiologist and author of "Good Health for African Americans."

Clifton & Damita Christopher   Sonya Taylor   Michael & Michelle Morgan

WHAT'S THE PROBLEM AND WHY?

TOP 4 CAUSES OF DEATH

CAUSE	%	RANK
Heart Disease	24%	1
Cancer	20%	2
Cerebrovascular Disease	8%	3
Accidents (unintentional injuries)	5%	5
Heart Disease	23%	1
Cancer	21%	2
Cerebrovascular Disease	7%	5
Diabetes	5%	7

BREAKDOWN OF TYPES OF CANCER AMONG BLACK PEOPLE IN THE US

MALE	FEMALE
Prostate 37%	Breast 32%
Lung & bronchus 12%	Lung & bronchus 11%
Colon & rectum 9%	Colon & rectum 9%
Kidney & renal pelvis 6%	Uterine corpus 7%
Liver & inthrahepatic bile duct 4%	Pancreas 4%
Pancreas 4%	Kidney & renal pelvis 4%
Myeloma 3%	Myeloma 4%
Non-Hodgkin lymphoma 3%	Non-Hodgkin lymphoma 3%
Urinary bladder 3%	Thyroid 3%
Leukemia 3%	Leukemia 2%

The four most common cancers are prostate, breast, lung, and colon.
They account for over half of all cancers among African Americans.

"Black people have the highest death rate & shortest survival of any racial/ethnic group in the U.S for most cancers."

Learn more in "Cancer Facts & figures for African Americans 2022-2024" on cancer.org.

GENERAL TRENDS IN PHYSICAL BODY & RESPONSE ACCORDING TO RESEARCH

Researchers have noted some differences in the African American population, as compared to Causcasians (upon which most nutrition research has been conducted). These may not apply to everyone, as they are trends.

 PHYSICAL BODY STRUCTURE

-Higher bone density
-Higher skeletal weight
-Different distribution of fat
-Higher muscle mass
-Shorter cervical length (leads to higher premature births, low-birth weight babies, asthma & 3x more SIDS)

-Shorter body trunks, with longer extremities (Wagner, Hayward 2000)

DIFFERENT HANDLING NUTRIENTS 

-Higher calcium retention (leading to better bone density)
-Higher water retention (may explain why African American diet of choice is laxatives)
-Salt is processed differently (stored in the kidneys instead of released in sweat)
-1/3 lower absorption of UV light to convert to Vitamin D
-Higher lactose intolerance rates

 DIFFERENT BODY CHEMICAL RESPONSE

-Higher leptin concentrations (gene that leads to body fatness)
-Higher growth hormone concentrations (relevant to hormone-driven cancers)
-Higher resistance to malaria (nearly 100% of West Africans are duffy-group negative)
-Higher rates of Sickle Cell Disease (the same gene that prevents malaria causes SCD)
-Higher rates of Renin-Angiotension-Aldosterone System (RAAS) Hormone system mutation (CDC 2017)

OTHER REASONS FOR RACIAL DISPARITIES

-Lack of quality research on African American populations
-Less access to quality, healthy food
-Higher rates of poverty
-Less access to safe areas for outdoor exercise
-Medical professional bias & treatment biases
-Historical & multi-generational distrust of doctors
-Less education & awareness of teachers on differences in nutrition
-African American stress (all stress affects digestive enzymes which dictate how we process nutrients)

Note: This list when referencing "higher" and "lower" is compared to non-Hispanic white Americans. Most research up until the last 30 years focused on Caucasian men as the baseline.

1. Vitamin D Absorption

2. Lactose Intolerance

3. Salt Processing & Hypertension

4. African-American Stress

5. Sickle-Cell Disease

6. Obesity

Gabriel Thompson, Anthony Thompson, Joseph Thompson

1. VITAMIN D ABSORPTION

Recommended Daily Allowance:

Adults age 19-69 = 600 IU (15 mcg)   Over 70 = 800 IU (20 mcg) Upper Limit (do not consume above this level) = 4000 IU (100 mcg)

Vitamin D is very important in cellular function and building the immune system. When sun shines (UV rays) on the skin, cholesterol in our skin cells provides energy for Vitamin D synthesis.

African American skin has high amounts of melanin which blocks many of the UV rays from the sun, so they produce 1/3 less Vitamin D from sun exposure than lighter skinned Caucasians. This melanin also makes African Americans more protected from sun damage. (O'Callaghan and Kiely, 2017)

4 RECOMMENDATIONS FOR NATURAL APPROACH:

DISEASES TIED TO VITAMIN D DEFICIENCY
- Cardiovacular disease
- Diabetes
- Cancer
- Autoimmune diseases
- And more

(Walker 2021)

SYMPTOMS OF VITAMIN D DEFICIENCY TO LOOK OUT FOR:
- General fatigue
- Muscle ache
- Mood changes
- Pain in your bones

1. 90 mins of sunlight, 3x a week, baring face, arms & trunk in midday.
2. Eat mushrooms! They mimic the action of skin, converting UV rays into Vit D.
3. Increase intake of dark, leafy greens as they contain Vitamin K which aids in Vitamin D absorption.
4. Eat fortified non-dairy milks and orange juice, grains, cereals and bread. (Mayo 2021)

WHAT BOOSTS VITAMIN D ABSORPTION?

1. Combining vitamin D with foods that are high in magnesium: avocadoes, pumpkin seeds & almonds.

2. Supplementing vitamin D3 with K2.

VITAMIN D TAKE AWAY:
Strive for natural approaches to increase Vitamin D and reduce factors that inhibit absorption.

HEALTHFUL CALCIUM SOURCES

BEANS

Black Turtle Beans (1 cup, boiled)	103mg
Chickpeas (1 cup, canned)	78mg
Great Northern Beans (1 cup, boiled)	121mg
Kidney Beans (1 cup, boiled)	50mg
Lentils (1 cup, boiled)	37mg
Lima Beans (1 cup, boiled)	52mg
Navy Beans (1 cup, boiled)	158mg
Pinto Beans (1 cup, boiled)	82mg
Soybeans (1 cup, boiled)	175mg
White Beans (1 cup, boiled)	161mg

VEGETABLES

Broccoli (1 cup, boiled)	178mg
Brussel Sprouts (8 sprouts)	56mg
Butternut Squash (1 cup, boiled)	84mg
Celery (1 cup, boiled)	54mg
Collards (1 cup, boiled)	148mg
Green Beans (1 cup, boiled)	58mg
Kale (1 cup, boiled)	94mg
Onions (1 cup, boiled)	58mg
Sweet Potato (1 cup, boiled)	70mg

FRUITS

Figs (dried, 10 medium)	269mg
Navel Oranges (1 medium)	56mg
Orange Juice, calcium fort (1 cup)	300mg*
Raisins (2/3 cup)	53mg

OTHER

English Muffin	92mg
Tofu (1/2 cup)	258mg
Wheat Flour, calcium enriched (1 cup)	238mg

*Package information. Source: Pennington JAT. Bowes and Church's Food Values of Portions Commonly Used. New York, Lippincott, 1998

2. LACTOSE INTOLERANCE

It is estimated that up to 70% of African Americans are lactose intolerant. "Lactase persistence" is an "abnormal" genetic trait carried by many caucasians. Most people of every other race (and every other mammalian species) do not carry that trait and are intolerant to lactose in adulthood. Interracial procreation has increased the number of African Americans able to tolerate dairy.

SYMPTOMS OF LACTOSE INTOLERANCE

-Diarrhea -Nausea/vomiting
-Stomach cramps -Bloating and gas
-Long-term inflammation
-Irritation of the digestive system can inhibit the way nutrients are absorbed and the delicate enzymatic and microbiome balance of the digestive system.

ONE THEORY

"Lactose intolerance in African Americans may be due to a genetic design. Research has shown that the proportion of people that are lactose intolerant can be tied to their region of genetic origin. Put simply, regions where dairy herds could be raised safely and efficiently produced people that could digest lactose."
– Dr. Greg Hall

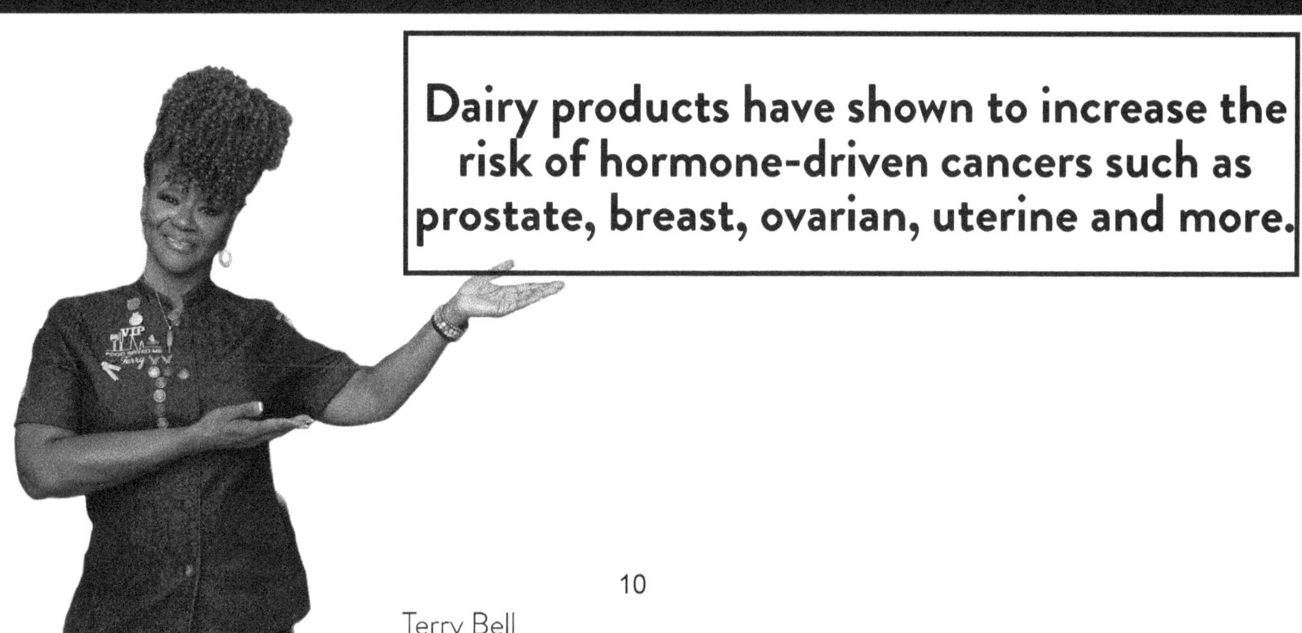

Dairy products have shown to increase the risk of hormone-driven cancers such as prostate, breast, ovarian, uterine and more.

Terry Bell

African Americans are at higher risk of getting and dying from hormone driven cancers. Dairy products tend to be high in estrogen, especially cheese. Added estrogens can increase the risk of cancers of the breast, prostate, ovary, uterus and more.
Dairy products are also higher in fat, generally speaking, which can add extra body weight which facilitates the production of more estrogen.
They also stimulate the production of IGR-1, a potent prostate cancer stimulus.
The galactose in dairy products has shown to attack the germ cells in the ovaries which eventually were supposed to become eggs. (Barnard 2020)

> ## There is a direct correlation of dairy intake and ovarian cancers, across 27 countries.

DAIRY PRODUCTS ARE OFTEN HIGH IN SATURATED FATS WHICH HAVE SIGNIFICANT IMPLICATIONS FOR:

1. Heart disease risk (by stimulating the liver to over-produce cholesterol) (Esselstyn 2008)
2. Alzheimer's disease (increasing risk dramatically) (Barnard 2014)

DAIRY SOURCES OF CALCIUM FAT CONTENT G/100G	EXCELLENT, MUCH HEALTHIER ALTERNATIVES
Milk 2.5	Dark leafy greens
Yogurt 1.7	Beans
Cheese 20.3	Almonds
Cream cheese 29.7	Oranges
Butter 52.1	Sesame Seeds
	Most non-dairy milk and orange juices are fortified with Calcium

TAKE AWAY:

Perhaps African Americans were not created genetically to consume lactose and this may be why the most common cancers in the African American population are hormone-driven.

3. SALT AND HYPERTENSION

HYPERTENSION

Hypertension is high blood pressure defined as:
Systolic BP >= 130 mm Hg, Diastolic BP >= 80 mm Hg
75% of African-Americans develop high blood pressure by age 55
(2x higher rate than Caucasians).

WHAT'S THE DEAL WITH SALT?

Caucasians release excess sodium through salt sweat and urine. Some researchers have concluded that African Americans do the reverse: their kidneys retain salt. (Morris 2005) While initially helpful in surviving the torrid temperatures in Africa, this has now become a disadvantage. So, a salt-sensitive people now also eat the highest levels of salt. (Wigertz 2005) Consider kidney disease; 13% of the U.S. population is African American, yet they account for over 35% of kidney dialysis patients.

"The body is designed to use the sodium it needs and get rid of the excess. Safety mechanisms are built into the body's systems to filter excess sodium through the kidneys and dump it out of the body via urine. If this system fails (as it apparently does in most AAs), the kidneys hold on to the excess sodium. The sodium attracts and retains water, which makes blood volume rise, which creates increased blood pressure and heart rate."
- Barbara M. Dixon, LDN, RD

This has more recently been discovered as a genetic predisposition of a hormone system called Renin-Angiotension-Aldosterone System (RAAS) that regulates blood pressure and fluid balance. When African Americans consume too much salt, it inappropriately stimulates the RAAS to retain salt and fluids.
(Walker 2020)

HOW MEDICATIONS MAY BE DIFFERENT

According to the American Heart Association, certain medications may be more effective for African Americans. For example, thiazide-type diuretics (water pills) and/or calcium channel blockers have shown to be more effective for African Americans, rather than typical medications recommended for caucasians.

SOURCES OF SATURATED FAT IN THE AMERICAN DIET

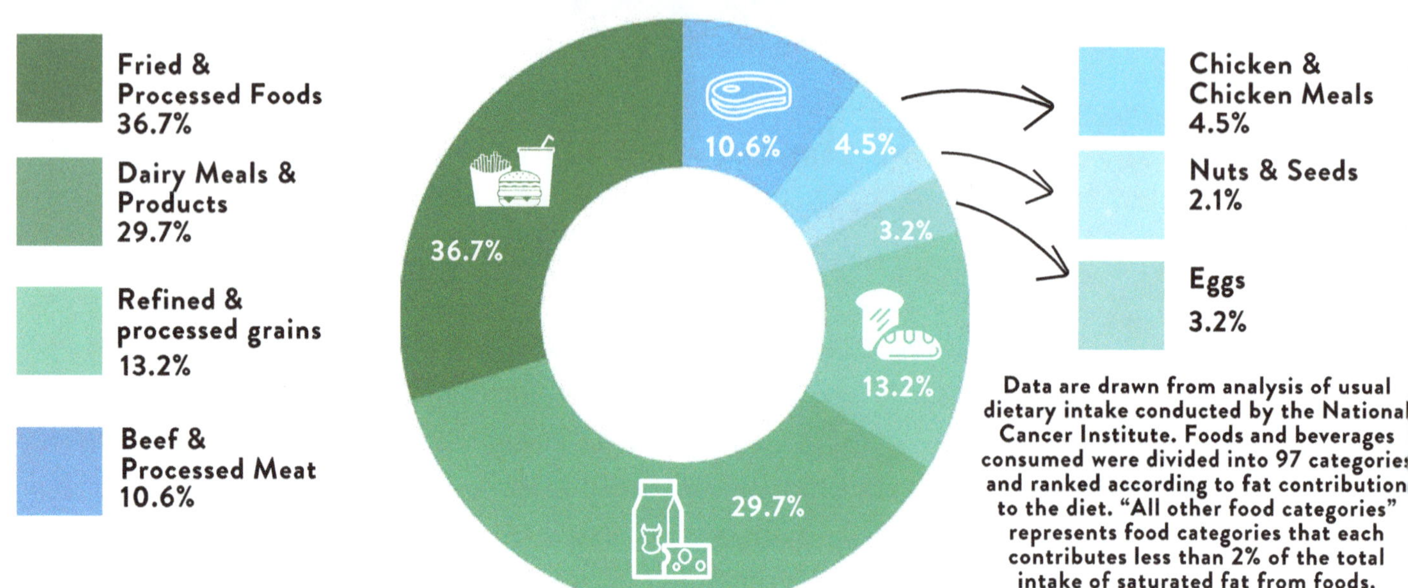

Data are drawn from analysis of usual dietary intake conducted by the National Cancer Institute. Foods and beverages consumed were divided into 97 categories and ranked according to fat contribution to the diet. "All other food categories" represents food categories that each contributes less than 2% of the total intake of saturated fat from foods.

EAT MORE PLANT-BASED MEALS TO LOWER BLOOD PRESSURE

-Plant based diets reduce risk of hypertension by 34%
-Fiber is only found in plants and it carries away excess cholesterol in the bloodstream and naturally lowers blood pressure

-Plant foods are cholesterol free
-Most are very low in saturated fat, if any
-Plants are naturally low in sodium

EAT MORE POTASSIUM-RICH FOODS:

Potassium-rich plant foods lower blood pressure by:
1. Relaxing blood vessels
2. Excreting sodium through the urine (Harvard 2022)

Dried Fruits	Beet Greens
Beans	Avocado
Lentils	Red Cabbage
Potatoes	Bananas
Winter Squash	Cantaloupe
Broccoli	Oranges
Spinach	Tomatoes
Cashews	Almonds

TAKE AWAY:

Most high-blood pressure is preventable through diet & lifestyle changes. Cook meals at home more using fresh, non-processed ingredients, focusing on plant foods. Cook without adding salts and oils to your food. High-blood pressure is no genetic, salt sensitivity is...

CHOLESTEROL & FAT'S RELATIONSHIP TO BLOOD PRESSURE

The Journal of National Medical Association conducted a cross-sectional analysis on fat intake. They concluded that African Americans consume an average of 86 grams of fat each day and 24 grams of it is saturated. According to the American Heart Association, we should target a diet that has no more than 5% of its total calories from saturated fats. For a 2,000 calorie diet, this equates to only 12-13 gr/day, max.

SATURATED FATS

While cholesterol is only found in animal foods, foods high in saturated fat can stimulate the liver to produce more cholesterol. High levels of saturated fat and cholesterol may contribute to increases in blood pressure through the development of plaques on vessel walls, which result in the reduction of both their diameter and elasticity.

According to Harvard Nutrition School,

"Saturated fat is mainly found in animal foods, but a few plant foods are also high in saturated fats, such as coconut, coconut oil, palm oil, and palm kernel oil." (Harvard, 2022)

The following table shows the amount of saturated fat in most oils:

Oil/Fat Source -% Saturated Fat

ANIMAL FATS	TROPICAL OILS	VEGETABLE OILS
Beef Tallow = 50%	Coconut Oil = 87%	Cottonseed Oil = 26%
Pork Fat (Lard) = 39%	Palm Kernel Oil = 82%	Peanut Oil = 17%
Chicken Fat = 30%	Palm Oil = 49%	Soybean Oil = 15%
		Sesame Oil = 14%
		Corn Oil = 13%
		Olive Oil = 13%
		Canola Oil = 12%
		Safflower Oil = 9%

CHOLESTEROL & FAT'S RELATIONSHIP TO BLOOD PRESSURE

TRANS FATS

Trans fats are the worst type of fats for the heart, blood vessels and rest of the body.

They have shown to:

Create inflammation
Lower immunity
Contribute to insulin resistance
Raise "bad" LDL cholesterol
Lower "good" HDL cholesterol

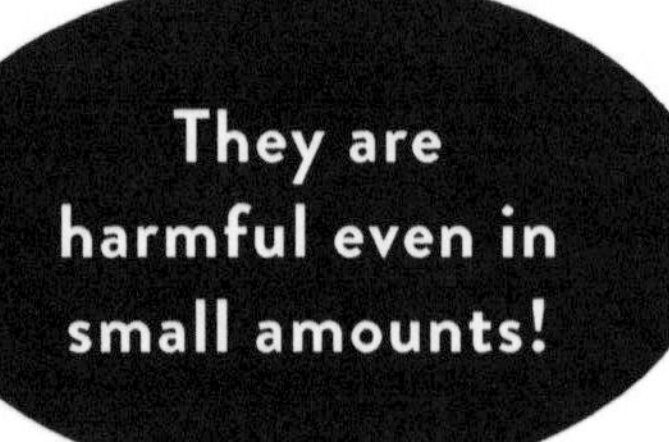

Trans fats are primarily found in:

- Partially hydrogenated oils*
- Most packaged foods
- Most fast food
- Most fast food

- Almost all fried foods
- Beef fat
- Dairy fat

*Hydrogenating the oil makes it last longer on the shelf and in high heat.

Americans should strive to remove trans fats from their diets.
Research shows for every additional 2% of calories from trans fats consumed daily, the risk of coronary heart disease increases by 23%.

For patients with heart disease, a diet of less than 10% of calorie from fat is recommended.

Note: Per current regulations, a food can be marked as "trans fat free" if it has less than 0.5 grams of trans fat in one serving.
Pay attention to serving size.

COMPARISON OF ANIMAL FOODS TO PLANT FOODS

ANIMAL FOODS (3.5 OZ, 100G)

	Fat (% of Calories)	Cholesterol (mg)
Beef, bottom round, lean	37	86
Chicken, white meat, skinless	23	85
Pork Loin, lean	41	81
Salmon, Atlantic	40	71
Trout, Rainbow	35	69
Tuna, White	21	42

PLANT FOODS

	Fat (% of Calories)	Cholesterol (mg)
Beans, Navy	4	0
Broccoli	11	0
Lentils	3	0
Apple	3	0
Orange	4	0
Rice, Brown	7	0

Source: USDA, Agricultural Research Service Nutrient Data Laboratory

Foods Rich in Unsaturated Fats (it converts to Omega-3)

Chia, Flax & Hemp Seeds
Avocados
Broccoli
Walnuts, Pecans, Pistachios
Nut butters
Olives
Spirulina
Soybeans/Tofu
Dark Leafy Greens

Foods Rich in Saturated Fats

Beef
Pork
Lamb
Cheese
Milk
Other Dairy
Coconut Oil
Lard

Foods Rich in Trans Fats

Fried Foods
Snack Foods
Microwave Popcorn
Hydrogenated Oils

NOTES ON SALT PROCESSING & HYPERTENSION

4. AFRICAN AMERICAN STRESS

When we experience stress, our adrenal glands release cortisol. While cortisol is good to help us deal with immediate threats, eventually it will slowly break down muscle tissue. Adrenal glands were not designed for constant use.

When we are under frequent stress, physical changes occur in our bodies: (Brazier 2017)

The body shifts its fuel source and starts to burn carbs & sugar for fuel, instead of fat. This results in more stored fat and cravings for carbs and sweets.	Inhibits the body's ability to enter "delta" sleep, which is the phase where it restores & regenerates itself (which, in turn, releases more cortisol)
Difficulty maintaining hormone and fluid levels, which compromise nutrient absorption.	Compromises the immune system, leaving us more susceptible to serious disease.

More African American men die from heart attacks related to stress than any other ethnic group in the U.S. African American women over 55 have the second highest rate of heart attacks related to stress. (Walker 2020)

"Experts now believe that the ordinary daily hassles that many African Americans must live with cause more stress than major life events."
– Cynthia Dixon, MD

As racism persists, many African Americans have more fear and suppressed rage. Studies show that people who have the most control over their lives experience less stress… racism deprives people of control. When poverty is also involved, frustration and stress levels increase even more.

Proven Stress Busters:
Breathing exercises | Healthy Diet (w/probiotics) | Meditation & Prayer | Regular exercise & long walks | Music | Yoga | Talking it out | Hot bath

TAKE AWAY:
Being aware of and recognizing stress is important.
We must take extra steps to manage our stress levels.
Diet is a great start.

NOTES ON AFRICAN AMERICAN STRESS

5. SICKLE CELL DISEASE (SCD)

The same gene that prevents malaria is the one that causes Sickle Cell Disease.
SCD is a genetic trait passed down through parents.
If one parent has the gene, the child will have *Sickle Cell Trait,* which is usually asymptomatic.
If both parents have the gene, the child will have *Sickle Cell Disease.* (CDC 2020)

About 1 in 12 African-Americans have Sickle Cell Trait.
SCD is a blood disease where red blood cells are deformed (in a sickle shape) and can block blood vessels. This creates blockages, oxygen shortages, nutrient deficiencies and, often, pain. Patients with SCD have greater-than-average requirements for both calories and micronutrients. (PCRM Nutrition Guide for Clinicians 2020)

According to Physician's Committee for Responsible Medicine,

"A diet emphasizing fruits, vegetables, whole grains, and legumes will provide a greater proportion of essential nutrients than a typical Western diet, and appropriate supplementation (1-3 times the recommended intakes for most essential nutrients) can prevent deficiency and may decrease the likelihood of disease exacerbation."

SCD PATIENTS OFTEN DISPLAY A DEFICIENCY OF:
Vit A & carotenoids
Vitamin B6
Vitamin C
Vitamin E
Magnesium
Zinc

Studies show that supplementing with these nutrients can reduce the percentage of irreversibly sickled cells.

Also, Omega-3 fatty acids increase the fluidity of red blood cell membranes, which may prevent sickle cell crisis. In a small double-blind, placebo-controlled study, supplemental EPA and DHA had significant therapeutic benefits including reduction of severe anemia.

Hydrate well and often with water. Avoid alcohol and caffeine.

Iron is very dangerous for sickle cell patients.

Too much iron is extremely dangerous and causes damage to blood vessels, red blood cells, liver, hormone producing glands and heart. It is very difficult to know what damage due to iron overload in sickle cell patients because the sickle cell disease itself causes organ damage to the same organs affected by iron.

"The most healthful sources of iron are the same foods that bring you calcium: beans and green leafy vegetables. They are rich in iron but carry it in a special form called non-heme iron. Your body easily absorbs this form when its in need of more iron, but the iron passes harmlessly out of the body when you have all you need. In contrast, meats contain heme-iron, which is like an uninvited guest at your party: it barges in whether you need it or not. Over the long-run, meat eaters tends to accumulate too much iron."

\- Excerpt from "Dr. Neal Barnard's Program for Preventing & Reversing Heart Disease."

FOOD SOURCES OF SCD NUTRIENT DEFICIENCIES

Vitamin A and carotenoids – dark, leafy greens, sweet potato, pumpkin, carrots, mango, cantaloupe, red bell pepper

Vitamin B6 – chickpeas, fortified cereals, dark,leafy greens, bananas, papayas, oranges, canteloupe

Vitamin C – kiwi, orange, lemon, lime, bell peppers, strawberries, white potatoes, cruciferous vegetables

Vitamin E – mango, spinach, asparagus, avocado, nuts, seeds, collard greens

Magnesium – almonds, cashews, flax seeds, peanuts, beans, quinoa, spinach, dark chocolate

Zinc – beans, tofu, lentils, nuts, rice, mushrooms, avocadoes, asparagus

TAKE AWAY:

Diet matters for Sickle Cell Disease. We should focus more on micronutrients, which are found in fruits and vegetables. Also, we need iron from non-heme sources.

Citrus Fruits 

Loaded with Vitamin C to boost the immune system.

Berries 

High in fiber, berries are naturally sweet, and their rich colors mean they are high in antioxidants and disease-fighting nutrients.

Tomatoes

These are high in vitamin C and lycopene, which has been shown to reduce the risk of prostate cancer. A cooked tomato has about 4 times more lycopene than a raw tomato.

Carrots, Sweet Potato, Mango & Pumpkin

Rich source of Vitamin A (Beta-Carotene) which has shown helps prevent Breast Cancer, improve eye sight and boost the immune system.

Leafy Greens 

Dark, leafy greens are a good source of vitamin A, vitamin C, and calcium, as well as several phytochemicals (chemicals made by plants that have a positive effect on your health). They also add fiber into the diet.

Celery

Lutein promotes colon health.

Apples

Vitamin C and anti-inflammatory.

Allium

Anti-cancer properties and reduce inflammation. These include garlic, onions, leeks, scallions, chives, and shallots. Pro tip: Always cut your garlic at least 10 minutes before you heat it to preserve the cancer-fighting allicin in it.

But what about protein??

Good news - ALL whole plant foods have protein! Beans = yes! Grains = yes! Fruits = yes! Veggies = yes! Nuts & Seeds = yes, yes!

Aim for at least 5 servings of fruits and vegetables per day!

"Harvard recommends at least half of our plate be filled with fruits and vegetables!"

NOTES ON SICKLE-CELL DISEASE

6. OBESITY

THE LEPTIN ISSUE

Obese African-American women often have higher leptin concentrations – a gene that (when the person has leptin resistance) leads to body fatness. (Nicklas 1997)

Leptin resistance can lead to overeating and excess fat storage because brain receptors are resistant. (Kaze 2021)

Other health problems can mess with your leptin signaling too. For example, chronic inflammation and high levels of triglycerides (a kind of fat found in your blood) can make it harder for leptin to cross the blood-brain barrier.

HOW TO OVERCOME OBESITY
(AND HORMONE DRIVEN CANCERS)

1. Eat foods lower in fat
2. Avoid using added oils
3. Set aside dairy products (these increase estrogen)
4. Increase fiber to 40 grams per day
5. Exercise 1-hour per day, a brisk walk at minimum
6. Eat more poly & mono unsaturated fats vs saturated fats
7. Eliminate trans-fat intake
8. Reduce going out to eat and eating processed foods

Plant sources of poly & mono-unsaturated fats:

-Avocado
-Olives
-Nuts & nut butters
-Seeds

GOOD NEWS! All of these nutrition guidelines to reduce body weight have also shown to protect us from the most common diseases listed above!

6. OBESITY CONT

Obesity is the leading controllable risk factor for:

- Heart Disease
- Diabetes
- Surgical Complications
- Hormone-driven Cancers
(breast, prostate, ovarian, uterine)

- Arthritis
- Fatty Liver
- Gallstones
- Infertility
- Many more...

HOW IS FAT RELATED TO CANCER?

**Excess body fat is an estrogen-producing factory. (Barnard 2020)
This excess estrogen increases risk of:**

> 1. Reproductive Issues (infertility, PCOS, PMS, endometriosis)
> AND
> 2. Hormone-driven cancers (prostate, breast, ovarian, uterine)

Meats, dairy products, oils and fried foods tend to be the highest fat foods. Whole plants (like beans, whole grains, fruits and vegetables) tend to be significantly lower in fat, with the exception of nuts and seeds.

LET'S TALK OIL!

**ALL oils are 100% fat, and are a mixture of saturated & unsaturated fats.
Oil has no fiber or protein in it.**

Instead of oil we recommend:

**1) Cooking vegetables in a small amount of broth & using the lid, to minimize sticking.
2) If seeking health benefits, like Omega 3s, eat the whole food instead of the extracted oil.
Example: Eat an olive instead of olive oil.**

BMI standards and thresholds can be inaccurate for African Americans and these affect diagnoses, health insurance premiums and more.

A recent study suggests about 75 million adults in the United States are being misclassified as healthy or unhealthy based on their BMI alone.

African Americans have significantly denser bones, larger bone structure, higher muscle mass and different distribution of weight. BMI charts can be wildly inaccurate for African Americans and these affect diagnoses, health insurance premiums and more…

Dr. Fatima Cody Stanford, MD, MPH is a leading obesity medicine doctor at Massachussetts General Hospital is Boston and is a black woman. She and her colleagues calculated and proposed different BMI standards that became published in the Mayo Clinic Proceedings. (Everyday Health, 2022)

PROPOSED BMI RANGES FOR THE BIPOC COMMUNITY

WOMEN			MEN			OBESITY CORMOBIDITY
WHITE	HISPANIC	BLACK	WHITE	HISPANIC	BLACK	
27	28	31	29	29	28	Hypertension
25	27	29	27	26	27	Dyslipidemia
29	30	33	30	29	29	Diabetes
28	30	31	29	29	28	≤ 2 risk factors
27	29	31	29	28	28	Average

Source: Source: Mayo Clinic Proceedings (2019)

6. OBESITY & BMI CONT

"We looked at the current data from the National Health and Nutrition Examination Survey, known as NHANES, and analyzed that data for weight status, race, ethnicity, gender, and certain risk for obesity-related diseases like diabetes, high blood pressure, [and] high cholesterol, and were able to delineate what the [BMI] cutoffs would be with adjustments," she explains.

Stanford went on to explain that black people tend to have more subcutaneous fat, which lies just below the surface of the skin, in the hip, buttock and thigh regions, while white people tend to carry more fat around the organs, known as visceral fat. Of the two, visceral fat poses a higher risk to metabolic health. It is linked to insulin resistance and carries a higher risk of death. Meanwhile, subcutaneous fat carries less risk, and a few studies have suggested it can lower the risk of type 2 diabetes.

Further, Black people may have less body fat and more lean muscle mass than white people at the same BMI. Black women seem to be most negatively affected by current BMI recommendations. Stanford and her team show that obesity actually happens at a higher BMI than it does for women of other races.

Amber Charles Alexis, MSPH, RDN has extensively reviewed the disparity in BMI for black women and offers 3 alternative health metrics aside from BMI that may be more accurate.

These explore:
1.Waist circumference

2. Waist to Hip Ratio (WHR)

3. BIA

Check out the article for more information and discuss options with your doctor. Waist circumference is a independent predictor of heart disease and type 2 diabetes risk. WHR is also a strong predictor of metabolic risk and heart disease.

https://www.ncbi.nlm.nih.gov/pmc/articles/PMC6078643/

https://pubmed.ncbi.nlm.nih.gov/31930817/

https://pubmed.ncbi.nlm.nih.gov/31930817/

NUTRIENT COMPOSITION OF PLANT & ANIMAL-BASED FOOD

FROM DR. T. COLIN CAMPBELL, AUTHOR OF THE CHINA STUDY

(PER 500 CALORIES OF ENERGY)

 VS 

NUTRIENT	PLANT-BASED FOODS*	ANIMAL-BASED FOODS**
Cholesterol (mg)	——	137
Fat (g)	4	36
Protein (g)	33	34
Beta-carotene (mcg)	29,919	17
Dietary Fiber (g)	31	——
Vitamin C (mg)	293	4
Folate (mcg)	1,168	19
Vitamin E (mg_ATE)	11	0.5
Iron (mg)	20	2
Magnesium (mg)	548	51
Calcium (mg)	545	252

* Equal parts of tomatoes, spinach, lima beans, potatoes

** Equal parts of beef, pork, chicken whole milk

NOTES ON OBESITY

HOW DIABETES RELATES TO OBESITY IN THE AFRICAN AMERICAN CULTURE

A study conducted by Northwestern University Feinberg School of Medicine, with over 4,200 participants, explored this disparity. The researchers concluded that only a small amount of the disparity could be attributed to neighborhood, psychosocial, socioeconomic, and behavioral risk. The primary contributor to increased risk was biological risk factors such as, body mass index, waist measurement, fasting glucose levels, lipids, blood pressure, and lung function.

3 RULES FOR REVERSING OR PREVENTING TYPE 2 DIABETES:

1. Avoid animal products (this includes meat, dairy, eggs and fish) as these tend to be much higher in fat than whole, plant foods.

2. Eliminate or minimize added oils because they are 100% fat.

3. Favor high-fiber, low-glycemic foods.

Fiber is important for diabetes prevention and reversal and is only found in plants. Fiber can help control blood sugar. Because the body cannot absorb and break down fiber, it does not cause a spike in blood sugar the way other carbohydrates can. This lack of breaking down causes it to move slowly through the stomach, providing a longer lasting feeling of fullness. As an added bonus, most foods that are high in fiber are also low in fat and calories. (CDC 2021).

With increase in fiber, a decrease in hemoglobin, fasting blood sugar, insulin resistance, total cholesterol, low-density lipoprotein (LDL), triglycerides, body weight, body mass index, and C-reactive protein was observed.
This is across all types of diabetes and all sources of dietary fiber.
(Reynolds, Ackerman, Mann 2020)

 Have Type 1 Diabetes?

Guess what! These rules work for you too to reduce your insulin requirements by up to 60%. Many studies confirm that high-fiber diets result in improved glycemic control for Type 1 diabetes as well. In one study, two multi-country cohorts of adults were followed for over 8 years. The results observed were astounding!

TAKE AWAY:
Maintaining a healthy weight, along with a diet rich in fiber, can dramatically lower risk of Type 2 Diabetes.

HOW DIABETES RELATES TO OBESITY IN THE AFRICAN AMERICAN CULTURE CONT

Diabetes is a disease that occurs when blood glucose (also called blood sugar) is too high. Over time, it can cause nerve damage, eye problems, kidney disease and heart disease. Insulin is made by the pancreas and it helps glucose get into the cells to be used for energy. When fat builds up inside the cell, it prevents insulin from doing its job. Subsequently, the pancreas makes more and more insulin trying to overcome this resistance. If it cannot keep up, glucose builds up in the blood, raising blood sugar levels. (Barnard 2007)

Although it can occur at any age, patients in middle-age or over that are overweight or obese are most likely to develop Type 2 diabetes. (NIH 2018)

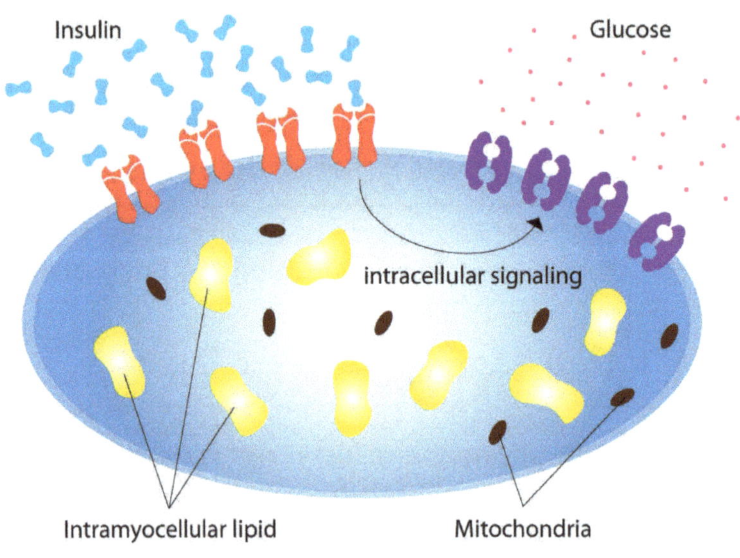

Here is the process as described in "Dr. Neal Barnard's Program for Reversing Diabetes" by Dr. Neal Barnard:

"Normally, insulin attaches to receptors on the cell's surface and signals the cell membrane to allow glucose to enter. However, if fat, called intramyocellular lipid, accumulates inside the cell, it interferes with insulin's intracellular signaling process. Tiny organelles, called mitochondria, are supposed to burn fat, and their failure to keep up with accumulating fat may be the origin of Type 2 diabetes. Luckily, evidence shows that diet changes can reduce the amount of fat inside the cell."

According to the National Institutes of Health, African Americans are 60% more likely to develop Type 2 diabetes than non-Hispanic Caucasians.

FIBER

Fiber is beneficial for disease prevention because it helps to:

Regulate Blood Sugar

Remove excess Cholesterol

Remove excess Hormones

Remove Carcinogens and Toxins

Shuttle waste out of the body

Aid in Digestion

Aids in weight loss and provide "full" feeling

Helps foster a healthy gut microbiome

Goal >40 Grams per Day

Fiber is only found in plants or supplements from plants.

Fiber Estimates in Common Foods:

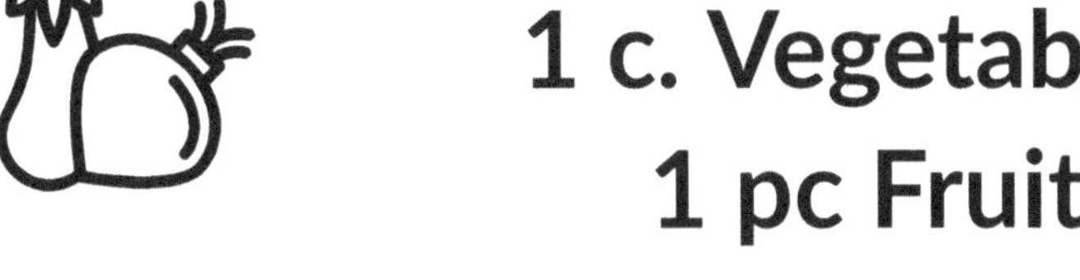

1 c. Beans ~ 14 g.
1 c. Whole Grain ~ 5 g.
1/2 c. Nuts ~ 5g.
1 c. Vegetables ~ 4 g.
1 pc Fruit ~ 3 g.

***Beans are a fiber powerhouse!**
They are also rich in protein, iron, calcium and folate.

THE GREAT AFRICAN DIET SWAP

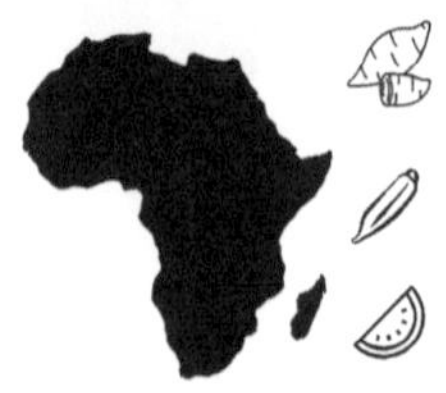

There is extensive experimental evidence that the products of fiber fermentation, in particular butyrate, are anti-inflammatory and have a protective, anti-cancer effect on the colon. In contrast, research also shows there is a promotional effect of dietary fat on colon cancer cells by stimulating bile acid synthesis from the liver.

Previously, studies on Japanese migrants to Hawaii have shown that it takes one generation of westernization to change their low incidence of colon cancer to the high rates observed in native Hawaiians.

As a follow-up, a landmark study was conducted by University of Pittsburgh and Imperial College London involving 20 African Americans and 20 participants from rural South Africa. African Americans are over 13 times more like to get colon cancer than rural Africans. The traditional Western (and African American) diet is high in fat and protein, but low in fiber. Therefore, this traditional diet is promoting colon cancer cells and contributes to colon cancer being the leading cancer in all Americans.

In contrast, the traditional rural African diet is very high in fiber and low in fat and protein. This high-fiber diet, creating large production of butyrate and minimizing the promoting effects of fat, contributes to much lower incidences of colon cancer in native African populations.

Both groups had colonoscopies before and after the diet swap. Before the swap, over half of the African Americans had polyps in their colon and higher rates of mucosal proliferation. Polyps are abnormal growth in the colon which may lead to colon cancer. None of the Africans showed polyps in their colon.

For two weeks, the African Americans ate a traditional South African diet and the South Africans ate a typical American diet.

In this short period of time, significant changes were observed. The American group showed increase in butyrate production, reduced biomarkers for cancer and suppression of secondary bile acid synthesis resulting in dramatically less inflammation. Unfortunately, the African group measured a significant increase in inflammation and all biomarkers related to colon cancer risk after only two weeks.

TAKE AWAY:

Fiber and fat content in the diet have a profound effect on colon microbiota within just days.

HIGH FIBER FOODS

FROM NUTRITIONTOFIT.COM. LINDSEY JANEIRO, RDN

FRUIT

Avocado (1 medium)	13.5gr
Guava (1 cup)	9.0gr
Raspberries (1 cup)	8.0gr
Blackberries (1 cup)	7.6gr
Asian pear (1 medium)	6.5gr
Wild blueberries (1 cup)	6.2gr
Passion fruit (1/4 cup)	6.1gr
Persimon (1 fuit)	6.0gr
Pear (1 medium)	5.5gr
Kiwi (1 cup)	5.4gr
Grapefruit (1 fuit)	5.0gr
Apple with skin (1 medium)	4.8gr
Starfruit (1 cup)	3.7gr
Orange (1 medium)	3.7gr
Dried figs (1/4 cup)	3.7gr
Blueberries (1 cup)	3.6gr
Pomegranate seeds (1/2 cup)	3.5gr
Mandarin orange (1 cup)	3.5gr
Tangerine (1 cup)	3.5gr
Banana (1 medium)	3.2gr
Apricots (1 cup)	3.1gr
Prune/dried plums (1/4 cup)	3.1gr
Strawberry (1 cup)	3.0gr
Dates (1/4 cup)	3.0gr
Cherries (1 cup)	2.9gr
Mango (1 cup)	2.6gr
Pineapple (1 cup)	2.3gr

VEGETABLES

Green peas (1 cup)	8.8gr
Pumpkin, pureed (1 cup)	7.0gr
Taro root, cooked (1 cup)	6.8gr
Sweet potato, cooked (1 cup)	6.4gr
Winter squash, cooked (1 cup)	6.4gr
Jicama (1 cup)	5.8gr
Yam, cooked (1 cup)	5.4gr
Broccoli, cooked (1 cup)	5.2gr
Cauliflower, cooked (1 cup)	5.0gr
Turnip greens, cooked (1 cup)	5.0gr
Carrots, cooked (1 cup)	4.8gr
Snow peas (1 cup)	4.6gr
Brussel sprouts, cooked (1 cup)	4.0gr
Potato with skin, baked	4.0gr
Carrots, raw (1 cup)	3.6gr
Sweet Corn (1 cup)	3.6gr
Red bell pep (1 cup)	3.2gr
Beets, cooked (1 cup)	2.8gr
Tomato, raw (1 medium)	1.0gr
Spinach, raw (1 cup)	0.7gr

GRAINS

Spaghetti, whole wheat, cooked (1 cup)	6.0gr
Barley, pearled, cooked (1 cup)	6.0gr
Bran flakes (3/4 cup)	5.5gr
Quinoa, cooked (1 cup)	5.0gr
Oat bran muffin (1 medium)	5.0gr
Oatmeal, instant, cooked (1 cup)	5.0gr
Pop corn, air-popped (3 cups)	3.5gr
Brown rice, cooked (1 cup)	3.5gr
Bread, whole-wheat (1 slice)	2.0gr
Bread, rye (1 slice)	2.0gr
White rice, cooked (1 cup)	1.0gr

LEGUMES

Navy beans, cooked (1/2 cup)	9.6gr
Small white beans, cooked (1/2 cup)	9.3gr
Split peas, cooked (1/2 cup)	8.0gr
Lentils, cooked (1/2 cup)	7.8gr
Black beans, cooked (1/2 cup)	7.5gr
Chickpeas, cooked (1/2 cup)	6.3gr
Great northen beans, cooked (1/2 cup)	6.2gr
White beans, cooked (1/2 cup)	5.7gr
Edemame, cooked (1/2 cup)	4.1gr
Turnip greens, cooked (1 cup)	5.0gr
Carrots, cooked (1 cup)	4.8gr

FATS

Pumpkin seeds (1oz)	5.2gr
Coconut (1oz)	4.6gr
Chia seeds (1 Tbsp)	4.1gr
Almonds (1 oz)	3.5gr
Sunflower seeds (1 oz)	3.1gr
Hemp hearts, hulled (1 oz)	3.0gr
Pine nuts (1 oz)	3.0gr
Pistachios (1 oz)	2.9gr
Flax seeds (1 Tbsp)	2.8gr
Hazelnuts (1/4 cup)	2.8gr
Pecans(1 oz)	2.7gr
Peanut butter (1 oz)	2.1gr
Walnuts (1 oz)	2.0gr

FLAVORINGS

Cocoa powder (1 Tbsp)	2.0gr
Cinnamon (1 tsp)	1.4gr

FIBER FUN FACTS

1. PLANTS ARE A MIXTURE OF SOLUBLE & INSOLUBLE FIBER WITH DIFFERENT AMOUNTS DEPENDING ON THE FOOD

a. Soluble: helps to remove extra cholesterol, hormones and blood sugar. It also aids in digestion of nutrients.

b. Insoluble: softens the stool and helps usher waste out of the body, without straining the colon.

2. FIBER HELPS CONTROL CRAVINGS

Because most processed carbs have little to no fiber, they release sugar that floods the blood stream rapidly. The resulting insulin surge, and then crash, triggers a craving for more sugar. When we eat foods rich in fiber, the fiber holds onto the carbohydrate and slowly releases it over 2-3 hours. This slow release keeps blood sugar steady and staves off cravings.

3. FIBER PROTECTS HEART HEALTH

Soluble fiber binds with LDL, the "bad" cholesterol in the digestive system and moves it out of the body through waste. Fiber is only found in plants, which are typically much lower fat foods than animal products. Eating lower fat foods make the blood more viscous and less fatty, helping to lower blood pressure.

4. FIBER HELPS PREVENT DIABETES

Soluble fibers help to slow the absorption of sugar into the body. By slowing the digestion process, we have a more sustained conversion of the carbohydrates to glucose for the body to use as energy. This energy helps maintain steady insulin and energy levels.

FIBER FUN FACTS

5. FIBER PROTECTS FROM ALZHEIMER'S AND DEMENTIA

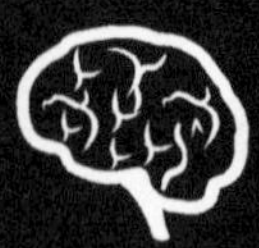

And it makes you smarter!
Microglia are a major type of immune cell in the brain. They tend to become hyperactive & chronically inflamed with age. This inflammation is one of the main causes of memory and cognitive decline in old age. Butyrate is a short-chain fatty acid that is produced in the colon when good bacteria ferment fiber in the gut. It can improve memory and reduce inflammation. Scientists have found that a high-fiber diet reduces inflammation n the brain's microglia! The researchers suspect that this was achieved by diminishing the production of a pro-inflammatory chemical known as interleukin-1B, which some studies have linked with Alzheimer's

6. FIBER PROTECTS AGAINST COLON CANCER

When good bacteria ferment fiber in the gut, they produce butyrate. Lots of it! Butyrate has an anti-cancer effect, killing off colon cancer cells and reducing inflammation. Measuring butyrate is a powerful biomarker of colon cancer risk. In research, dramatic changes in butyrate levels have been measured withn just two weeks of changing to a high-fiber diet.

Beware of fiber additives. We want to consume "intact" fiber, which is fiber in its original form, proven to have the most health benefits. Processed food companies are now adding isolated or synthetic fiber to foods so they can increase the fiber count on the nutrition label. Not all of these have been tested. And while some may have small benefits (primarily helping to move waste along), none has all of the benefits and have been proven to be safe for consumption. Whole foods are best! And, when eating a processed food, always read the nutrition & ingredient label.

SOY: MYTHS AND BENEFITS

According to the Mayo clinic,

Studies show that a lifelong diet rich in soy foods reduces the risk of breast cancer in women. This protective effect is less dramatic for women who eat less soy or who start eating soy later in life. Soy contains protein, isoflavones and fiber, all of which provide health benefits.

Soy is a phyto-estrogen (i.e. plant-estrogen). High levels of have been linked to an increased risk of breast cancer. However, soy contains such low levels of estrogen that they are actually protective. Soy attaches to estrogen receptors on a cells surface preventing the larger, more dangerous estrogens from attaching and changing the cell's chemistry. However, soy contains such low levels of estrogen that they are actually protective.

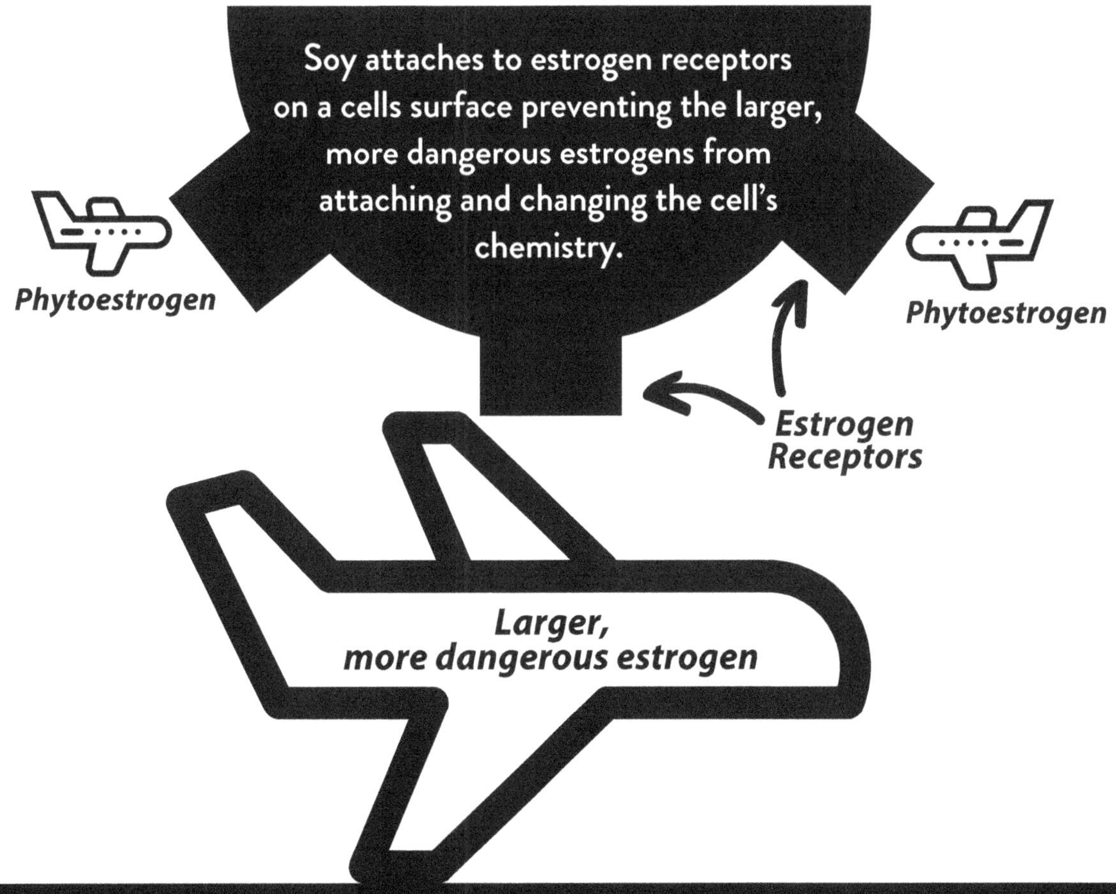

A popular study in the Chinese Journal of Cancer found that, "Soy food consumption, more popular in Asian populations, is associated with a 25% to 30% reduced risk of prostate cancer."

It is hypothesized that the isoflavones in soy products products women and men from hormone-driven cancers. Note: Isoflavones taken in supplement form have shown to increase risk. So always get them from whole or minimally-processed soy foods.

SOY: MYTHS AND BENEFITS CONT

A large, cross-sectional study published in Cancer Epidemiol Biomarkers & Prevention showed that,

"Soy intake during childhood, adolescence, and adult life was associated with decreased breast cancer risk, with the strongest, most consistent effect for childhood intake. "

WHAT ABOUT MEN'S FERTILITY

There is a persistent myth, made popular in the 1980s, that asserts that soy reduces testosterone, fertility and sperm production in men... essentially feminizing them. The men in this small study consumed 3 quarts of soymilk per day! Luckily, this has been disproven many times over. One of these was a large cross-sectional study which showed men who consume 1-2 servings of soy per day had significantly higher ejaculate volume. It is hypothesized that the isoflavones in soy products products women and men from hormone-driven cancers.

Best Sources of Soy are:

Miso
Edamame
Tofu
Tempeh
Soy milk (made from whole soy beans rather than powder).

Organic and non-GMO are the preferred options.

EVOLUTION OF THE AFRICAN AMERICAN DIET (OF ENSLAVED PEOPLE) FROM ITS ORIGINS TO NOW

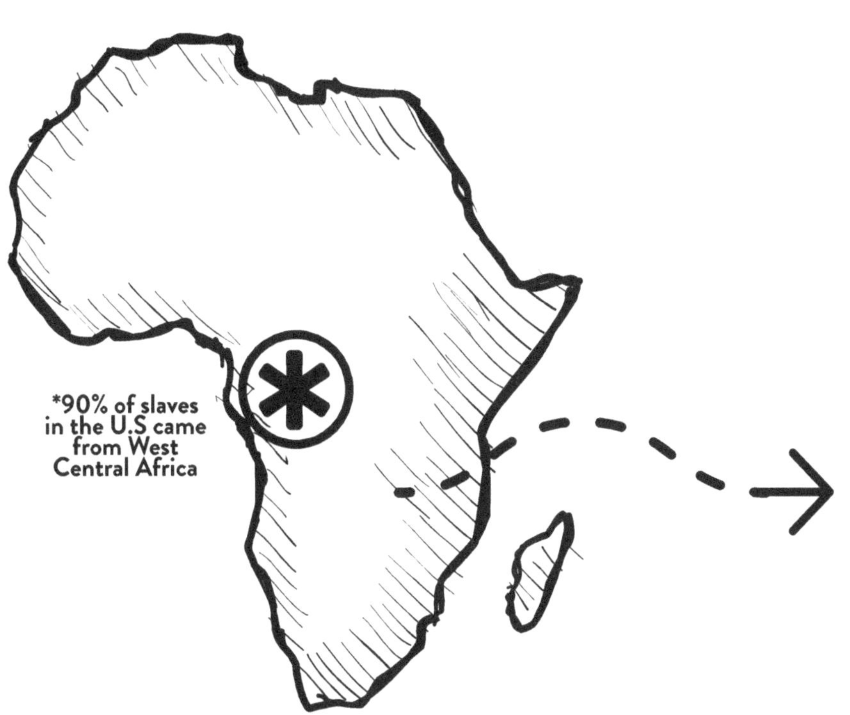

AFRICAN DIET

Almost fully plant-based diet
Very low-fat diet
Boiled food or fried in oil to give them more fat to survive in their environment
Yams, okra, black-eyed peas, taro, watermelon, sesame
Dairy products and Salt were not a part of the traditional African diet.

SHIP DIET
Corn & Nuts

40

Charolette & Kevin Washington   A.C Flye   JuNene K Katia Thompson

EVOLUTION OF THE AFRICAN AMERICAN DIET (OF ENSLAVED PEOPLE) FROM ITS ORIGINS TO NOW

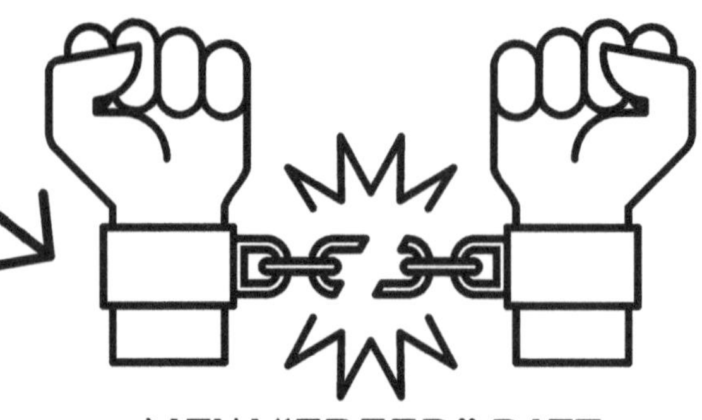

NEW "FREED" DIET

DIET OF ENSLAVED PEOPLE IN THE USA

"Soul Food" persisted but the intense labor/exercise did not
Newly freed African-Americans kept the meat in their diets and increased oil frying of meats
Where did the fruits & veggies go?
About 90% of African Americans(and all Americans in general) eat only 2 or less veggies a day.

One-pot dishes of corn, chitlins and leftover meat & vegetable scraps from plantation owners. High-calorie meals served a purpose for slaves to labor all day. Salt was introduced to the diet as a means to preserve meats.

African cultural elements and values were retained:

Extended family ties
Respect for elders
Respect for mothers
Sunday dinner is still a tradition

The Mathis Family
Family Reunion. Dallas, TX. Circa 1977

"Diabetes is not part of your heritage. Neither is heart disease. What is in your heritage is a healthy heart, strong body, extraordinary energy, vibrant and delicious foods, and a long, healthy life." - Oldwayspt.org

1. Consume 11-13 fruits and vegetables per day to maximize antioxidants and boost immune system.
2. Eat at least 40 grams of fiber per day from whole plant foods.
3. Minimize or eliminate dairy products, alcohol and all added oils.
4. Cook at home more, rather than going out to eat to reduce sodium intake.
5. Minimize exposure to carcinogens, including those from plastics, chemicals, processed meats, common cookware, pesticides, tobacco smoking and more.
6. Replace consumption of meat products with cholesterol-free, lower-fat plant foods.
7. Focus on good sources of "healthy" poly & mono-unsaturated fats.
8. Consume eight to ten glasses of water each day.

Murdock "Doc" and Vera Gibbs

John & Patricia Richardson

BENEFITS OF TRADITIONAL AFRICAN FOODS

YAMS
- Rich in antioxidants which has shown to reduce colon tumor growth
- Great source of manganese and potassium, which support healthy blood pressure and cardiovascular function
- High in fiber; aiding in digestion, weight loss, hormone regulation and toxin removal
- Orange varieties are high in Vitamin A/beta-carotene which helps prevent breast cancer
- Good source of vitamin C & copper, which boost the immune system and help red blood cell production

WATERMELON
- Contains citrulline, antioxidant which increases nitric oxide production, expanding blood vessels, lowering blood pressure & improving male sexual function
- Contains carotenoids & lycopene
- Helps us to stay hydrated
- Low-calorie
- High in Vitamin C

MILLET
- Ancient grain with more amino acids than most other whole grains
- Contains highest calcium content of all whole grains
- Good source of soluble fiber which helps lower cholesterol
- Rich in phenolic compounds which protect the body from oxidative stress and inflammation
- Rich in catechins which bind to heavy metals to remove from the body
- Ideal grain for people with diabetes – high in fiber and protein, with a low-glycemic index

DARK LEAFY GREENS
- Cruciferous vegetables, which have shown to arrest the reproduction of cancer cells
- Great source of Vitamin C to boost the immune system
- Vitamin A to benefit eyes and female reproductive organs
- Just 2 cups has 128% of RDA for Vitamin K which builds strong bones and protects from fracture

OKRA
- Rich in Vitamin K, C & A
- Versatile for eating: Raw, boiled, grilled, pickled & dried
- The mucilage (gel-like substance) helps fiber to remove excess cholesterol
- Rich in Folate

BLACK EYED PEAS
- Excellent, low-fat source of fiber and protein
- Complex carbohydrate helpful for brain function
- Good source of iron, Vitamin A, Vitamin K and absorbable calcium
- Improves digestion and waste/toxin removal

NOTES ON FIBER

RECIPES

HOPPIN' JOHN SALAD
INGREDIENTS:

1 1/2 cups cooked black-eyed peas, rinsed and drained
2 cups cooked brown rice
1 celery stalk, sliced
2 green onions, sliced
1 Tbsp finely chopped fresh parsley
¼ cup lemon juice
2 garlic cloves, crushed
2 small tomatoes, diced
Salt/pepper to taste (optional)

DIRECTIONS
1. Combine the black-eyed peas, rice, green onions, celery, tomatoes, and chopped parsley in a large bowl.
2. Mix the lemon juice, salt, and garlic. Pour over the salad and toss to mix.
3. Chill 1 to 2 hours before serving.

PULLED-NO-PORK JACKFRUIT SLIDERS
INGREDIENTS:

8 oz baby bella mushrooms, sliced
14oz shredded jackfruit (try to find in water instead of brine)
1/2 red onion, sliced
1 1/2 cups canned peaches or fresh peaches, chopped
1/2 tsp sea salt
1/4 cup dark brown sugar
3/4 cup vegan BBQ sauce
6 regular hamburger buns or 12 slider buns
1 cup fried onions (store bought)

NON-DAIRY MAC & CHEESE
INGREDIENTS:

4 cups uncooked macaroni pasta
2 cups unsweetened soy milk
1 cup low-sodium vegetable broth
3/4 cup nutritional yeast flakes
3/4 tsp. salt
1/2 tsp. dried mustard
1/4 tsp. paprika
1/8 tsp. garlic powder
1/16 tsp. turmeric
1/4 cup all-purpose flour
Black pepper to taste

DIRECTIONS
1. Cook macaroni in a large saucepan according to package directions. Drain pasta and set aside.
2. In a small saucepan, combine all remaining ingredients, except flour. Bring to a simmer over medium-high heat. Once the sauce is hot and bubbling, slowly add the flour and whisk until all lumps have dissolved.
3. Pour hot cheese sauce over pasta and serve.

DIRECTIONS
1. Add the mushrooms, jackfruit, onion and peaches to a skillet to sauté.
2. Cover and cook at simmer until tender (about 20-25 min)
3. Remove cover. Gently stir in salt, brown sugar and BBQ sauce until veggies are coated.
4. Cook, uncovered over medium heat for a few minutes until the sauce thickens.
5. Divide onto hamburger buns and add crispy fried onions on top!

RECIPES

NOT-TOO-DIRTY RICE:
ADAPTED FROM VEGAN SOUL KITCHEN

INGREDIENTS:

1 cup long-grain brown rice, soaked in water overnight
8 oz of seitan, chopped finely (or shredded jackfruit)
1 cup diced red onion
1 cup diced green bell pepper
1 celery stalk, peeled of string fibers and chopped finely
1 tsp paprika
1/2 teaspoon chilli powder
1/4 Tbsp cayenne
2 Tbsp tamari
1/4 lbs tempeh (half 8-oz package), crumbled
3 cloves of garlic, minced
2 1/4 cups veggie stock
1/4 minced fresh parsley
Freshly ground white pepper

DIRECTIONS

1. Drain the rice and set aside
2. In a kitchen towel or paper towel squeeze the seitan of its moisture and set aside.
3. In a medium-size saucepan over medium heat, combine the onion, bell pepper, celery, paprika, chili powder, cayenne and tamari and sauté, stirring often until vegetables are soft, about 5 minutes. Add seitan, garlic, and reserved rice and cook until fragrant, about 3 minutes.
4. Add the stock to the saucepan and stir well, scraping the bottom of the pan to release any solids. Bring to a boil, cover, reduce heat to low, and cook for 50 minutes, until most of the water has evaporated.
5. Remove from heat and steam with cover on for at least 10 minutes.
6. Stir in the parsley. Season with white pepper and tamari to taste and serve hot.

SKILLET CORNBREAD
FROM: VEGAN SOUL FOOD COOKBOOK

INGREDIENTS:
13.5-oz coconut milk
1 tsp apple cider vinegar
1 cup of cornmeal
1 cup unbleached all-purpose flour
2/3 cup unsweetened applesauce
1/2 cup coconut sugar
1/4 cup coconut oil, melted
1 Tbsp baking powder
2 pinches of sea salt

DIRECTIONS

1. Preheat the oven to 350F.
2. In a measuring cup or small mixing bowl, combine the milk and vinegar, stir, and set aside.
3. In a large bowl, combine the cornmeal flour, applesauce, sugar, oil, baking powder, and salt and stir with a wooden spoon to combine.
4. Add the milk mixture and mix well
5. Into a large-skillet or oiled baking pan, pour the cornbread mixture and gently flatten with a wooden spoon.
6. Bake for 30 minutes or until the top is golden brown and the center is firm.
7. Take out of the oven and allow to cool for 5 minutes and serve.

TIP:

Add 1/2 cup of corn kernels, 1/2 cup of vegan shredded cheddar, and 1 diced jalapeño to add more bite and souther flair to this delicious corn bread.

OKRA & TOMATOES

INGREDIENTS:
24 oz can diced tomatoes
24 oz frozen okra
4-5 cloves garlic, Minced

DIRECTIONS

1. Add all ingredients to saucepan and turn to medium heat.
2. As it approaches a low boil, reduce heat to low and cook for 5-7minutes.
Do not overstir or overcook okra, as it can get very slimy.

KALE, WATERMELON & APPLE SALAD
FROM VEGAN SOUL FOOD BY NADIRA JENKINS-EL
INGREDIENTS:
For the dressing:
3 Tbsp white balsamic vinegar
2 Tbsp grapeseed or sunflower oil
1/2 tsp of agave nectar
1/2 tsp finely chopped fresh thyme
1/2 tsp sea salt, or more to taste
White pepper

For the salad:
1 1/2 bunches lacinato kale, stemmed, and cut
into thin ribbons
1/2 bunch of dandelion greens, roughly chopped
10 basil leaves, roughly chopped
1/3 cup red cabbage
1/4 cup thinly sliced onion
1 cup cubed ripe watermelon
1 cup peeled, diced apple
1/3 cup roasted cashews

DIRECTIONS
1. In a medium bowl, make dressing by
whisking together all the dressing
ingredients to combine
2. In a large bowl or individual serving bowls,
build the salad beginning with a mound of
kale and dandelion greens at the bottom,
then the basil, cabbage, and onions; and
finally the watermelon, apples, cashews, and
a drizzle of dressing.

WEST AFRICAN PEANUT STEW
FROM VEGAN SOUL FOOD BY NADIRA JENKINS-EL
INGREDIENTS:
1 cup diced onion
1 tsp peeled and minced fresh ginger
4 cloves of garlic, minced
1 1/2 cups diced sweet potatoes
1 tsp cumin
Sea salt
1 Habanero pepper
2 vegetable boullion cubes
4 cups warm water
3/4 cup chunky peanut butter
1 1/2 tsp sriracha (optional)
6 oz tomato paste
1 bunch of collard greens, stemmed and roughly chopped
1/2 cup of frozen corn
1/4 cup peanuts, roughly chopped
1/2 cup roughly chopped fresh parsley

DIRECTIONS
1. In a medium stockpot, heat the oil over
medium-high heat, then add the onions and ginger
and saute for 2-3 minutes.
2. Add the garlic, stir and sauce for another 1-2
minutes.
3. Add the sweet potatoes, cumin, salt to taste,
and whole Habanero pepper and saute for another
1-2 minutes.
4. Meanwhile, add the boullion cubes to the warm
water and stir to dissolve.
5. Add the dissolved bouillon, peanut butter,
sriracha (if using) and tomato paste to the
stockpot, and stir to combine. Cover, bring to a
soft boil, and then turn the heat to low.
6. Add the greens and corn and simmer for another
5-10 minutes or until the sweet potatoes and
collards are soft .
7. Remove Habanero and discard
Serve in bowl topped with the chopped peanuts
and fresh parsley.

CANDIED YAMS
INGREDIENTS:

6-8 medium sweet potatoes
1 cup brown sugar
1 lemon, juiced
1 tsp. ground ginger
1 tsp. vanilla
1 cup chopped pecans
Cinnamon (optional)
Nutmeg (optional)

DIRECTIONS
1. Cut washed, unpeeled potatoes in small cubes.
2. Add water and cook until tender enough to mash with a fork.
3. In a separate bowl, mix remaining ingredients.
4. Mash potatoes and top with pecan mixture. Cover and simmer for 5 minutes or until mixture is melted.

COLLARD GREENS AND VEGGIES
INGREDIENTS:

1 bunch collard greens, ribs removed and sliced into strips
1 medium onion, sliced
1 head garlic, minced
1 cup mushrooms, sliced
1 cup vegetable stock
2 Tbs. apple cider vinegar
Crushed red pepper & salt to taste

DIRECTIONS
1. Place garlic and onions in pan and turn to medium heat. Saute for 5-7 minutes or until lightly browned.
2. Add mushrooms, stock, apple cider vinegar and stir.
3. Add greens, crushed pepper and cover. Cook on medium heat until veggies reduce. Turn heat to low and cook for 20-30 minutes or until desired consistency.

DELICIOUS CHILLI BEANS
ADAPTED FROM #MSBRENDADEE ON YOUTUBE
INGREDIENTS:

1 lb. dried Pinto Beans
½ cup chopped Onions
½ cup chopped Bell Peppers
1 – 2 lbs Impossible Sausage
½ Tbsp Garlic Powder
½ Tbsp Onion Powder
Pepper to taste
2 15oz cans Tomato Sauce
2 Tbsp Chili Powder
½ Tbsp Cumin
½ Tbsp Sugar (optional)

DIRECTIONS

1. Soak beans in water overnight. Then, discard water and rinse.
2. Transfer beans to a large cooking pot. 3. Fill with water until the water level is about 2-3 inches above bean level.
4. Add half onions and bell peppers to the beans and bring to a low boil and cover.
5. Reduce heat to a rapid simmer on medium-low.
6. Check after an hour to make sure you have plenty of water.
7. Continue cooking for about 2 hours until beans are fork tender.
8. While waiting on the beans to cook, add remaining onions and bell peppers to a large skillet and cook over medium heat for 3-5 mins.
9. Add Impossible sausage to the skillet along with black pepper, garlic powder and onion powder. Cover and cover for 7-10 minutes, stirring occasionally until cooked through.
9. Once beans are tender, add sausage mixture to beans and mix gently.
10. Add tomato sauce, chili powder and cumin. Stir to mix well. Taste and season accordingly.
Add sugar, optionally, to cut the acidity of the tomatoes and create a richer taste.

RECIPES

PECAN SWEET POTATO PIE OATMEAL PARFAIT
CREDIT: LAILA ALI "FOOD FOR LIFE"

INGREDIENTS:

3/4 cup water, or dairy or nondairy milk, or a combination
1/2 cup rolled oats
2 tbsp fruit juice–sweetened dried cranberries or raisins
1/2 tsp ground cinnamon
Pinch of salt
1/2 cup mashed sweet potato
1 tbsp pure maple syrup
1/2 tsp pure maple extract (Optional)
1/2 tsp pure vanilla extract
1/2 cup plain Greek yogurt
1/4 cup toasted pecans, chopped

DIRECTIONS

1. Pour the water into a medium saucepan and bring to a boil over medium-high heat. Add the oats, cranberries, cinnamon, and salt, return to a boil, then reduce the heat and simmer for about 5 minutes, stirring only once or twice, until the oats begin to soften and the liquid thickens. Stir in the sweet potato and cook for about 2 minutes, until smooth and heated through. Add a little water if the oatmeal thickens too much. Turn off the heat and stir in the maple syrup, maple extract (if using), and vanilla. If you've got the time, cover and set aside for 5 minutes to absorb excess moisture and to bring all the flavors together.

2. To assemble the parfaits, pour one- quarter of the oatmeal into each of two parfait bowls or Mason jars. Top each with one-quarter of the yogurt, followed by one-quarter of the pecans. Repeat the layering, starting with oatmeal and ending with pecans. Serve immediately, or, if using Mason jars, cover and pop into your bag to take to your a.m. destination.

ZUCCHINI BOATS
BY JENNIFER FLORES

INGREDIENTS:

4 medium zucchini
1 tablespoon vegetable broth
1 white onion chopped
1 small bell pepper chopped (any color)
15 oz can of chickpeas drained and rinsed
4 tbsp milk, I use oat milk
2 tsp garlic powder
1/2 tsp smoked paprika
1/2 tsp cumin
1 bag (7oz) vegan cheese optional

DIRECTIONS

1. Preheat the oven to 350F.
2. Cut the zucchini in half (long ways) and scoop out the flesh leaving a thick border around the skin. You will need to keep the part you take out so you can set it aside it will be chopped up.
3. Heat broth in a pan over medium heat.
4. Add onion and sauté until onion until it becomes translucent.
5. Add bell pepper, zucchini flesh, all spices and milk. Cook for about 10 minutes, stirring occasionally, it will need to be tender.
6. Add chickpeas to the pan and cook for a few more minutes.
7. Stuff each zucchini half with the chickpea mix. If you desired, you can add vegan cheese on top and bake on 350degrees until cheese is melted, or about 25 minutes so the zucchini is tender.
Zucchini boats pair with a lot of sides. Chop up some veggies and sauté them, some black beans, side of quinoa or just alone.
Another option what I like to do and mix it up. I use quinoa instead of chickpea and follow the directions on the quinoa bag to make it.

RESOURCES WE LIKE

BOOKS:

Black Health Matters – Richard Walker, Jr, MD
Building Bone Vitality – Dr. Amy Lanou
Dr. Neal Barnard's Program for Reversing Diabetes - Dr. Neal Barnard
Good Health for African Americans - Barbara Dixon, LDN, RD
Prevent and Reverse Heart Disease – Dr. Caldwell Esselstyn
Power Foods for the Brain - Dr. Neal Barnard
The Cancer Survivor's Guide – Dr. Neal Barnard
The Cheese Trap – Dr. Neal Barnard
The China Study and Whole – Dr. T. Colin Campbell
Thrive – Brendan Brazier

COOKBOOKS:

But My Family Would Never Eat Vegan! – Kristy Turner
Food For Life – Laila Ali
Vegan Soul Food – Nadira Jenkins-El
Vegan Soul Kitchen – Bryant Terry
Vegan Cookbook for Kids – Barb Musick
Unbelievably Vegan - Charity Morgan

DOCUMENTARIES:

Forks Over Knives
Gamechangers
Seaspiracy
The Future of Food
What the Health

ONLINE CLASSES & RESOURCES

Foodsavedme.com
AAnutritionclass.com
Foodsavedme.institute

WE ENCOURAGE YOU TO EXPLORE THESE MORE ON YOUR OWN FOR A MORE IN-DEPTH UNDERSTANDING OF THE VARIETY OF TOPICS IN THE CLASS!

DeNoon, Daniel. (2017) Why 7 Deadly Diseases Strike Blacks Most: Health care disparities heighten disease differences between African-Americans and white Americans. https://www.webmd.com/hypertension-high-blood-pressure/features/why-7-deadly-diseases-strike-blacks-most

CDC (2017). Leading causes of death. https://www.cdc.gov/minorityhealth/lcod/men/2017/nonhispanic-black/index.htm

O'Callaghan, Karen M. and Kiely, Mairead E. (2017) Ethnic Disparities in the Dietary Requirement for Vitamin D During Pregnancy: considerations for nutrition policy and research. Proceedings of the Nutrition Society.

Walker, Richard W. Jr. MD. (2021) Black Health Matters. The vital facts you must know to protect your health and those of your loved ones. Square One Publishing.

Hall, Greg (2020). Lactose Intolerance in Africa Americans. https://drgreghall.com/2020/05/05/lactose-intolerance-african-americans/

Barnard, Neal (2020). Your Body in Balance: The New Science of Food, Hormones, and Health. Balance.

Morris, Maggie (2005). Purdue study finds races react differently to dietary salt, calcium. Purdue University. https://www.purdue.edu/uns/html4ever/2005/050510.Weaver.retention.html

Wigertz K, Palacios C, Jackman LA, Martin BR, McCabe LD, McCabe GP, Peacock M, Pratt JH, Weaver CM. Racial differences in calcium retention in response to dietary salt in adolescent girls. Am J Clin Nutr. 2005 Apr;81(4):845-50. doi: 10.1093/ajcn/81.4.845. PMID: 15817862.

Dixon, Barbara M. LDN.RD. (1994) Good Health for African Americans. Crown Publishers, Inc.

Wagner, Dale R and Heyward, Vivian H (2000) Measures of body composition in blacks and whites: a comparative review. American Journal Clinical Nutrition, 2000; 71-1392-402.

National Center on Birth Defects and Developmental Disabilities, Center for Disease Control and Prevention. (2020) 5 Facts You should know about Sickle Cell Disease.

https://www.cdc.gov/ncbddd/sicklecell/materials/infographic-5-facts.html

PCRM's Nutrition Guide for Clinicians. (2020) Sickle Cell Disease https://nutritionguide.pcrm.org/nutritionguide/view/Nutrition%20Guide%20for%0Clinicians/1342072/all/Sickle_Cell_Disease

Harvard T.H. Chan, School of Public Health. The Nutrition Source. (2022) Potassium https://www.hsph.harvard.edu/nutritionsource/potassium/

BIBLIOGRAPHY

Wang H, Chen W, Li D, Yin X, Zhang X, Olsen N, Zheng SG. Vitamin D and Chronic Diseases. Aging Dis. 2017 May 2;8(3):346-353. doi: https://doi.org/10.14336%2FAD.2016.1021

Robbins JM, Vaccarino V, Zhang H, Kasl SV. Excess type 2 diabetes in African-American women and men aged 40-74 and socioeconomic status: evidence from the Third National Health and Nutrition Examination Survey. J Epidemiol Community Health. 2000 Nov;54(11):839-45. doi: https://doi.org/10.1136/jech.54.11.839

Kolahdooz F, Butler JL, Christiansen K, Diette GB, Breysse PN, Hansel NN, McCormack MC, Sheehy T, Gittelsohn J, Sharma S. Food and Nutrient Intake in African American Children and Adolescents Aged 5 to 16 Years in Baltimore City. J Am Coll Nutr. 2016;35(3):205-16. doi: https://doi.org/10.1080%2F07315724.2014.959206 Epub 2015 Apr 9. PMID: 25856051; PMCID: PMC4888796.

Jardine, Meghan. (2018) Seven Reasons to Keep Saturated Fat Off Your Plate
https://www.pcrm.org/news/blog/seven-reasons-keep-saturated-fat-your-plate

Satia JA. Diet-related disparities: understanding the problem and accelerating solutions. J Am Diet Assoc. 2009 Apr;109 (4):610-5. doi: 10.1016/j.jada.2008.12.019 PMID: 19328255; PMCID: PMC2729116.

Sullivan, G. Michele. (2018) Short cervical length more common among black women, and more predictive of preterm birth https://www.mdedge.com/obgyn/article/158799/obstetrics/ short-cervical-length-more-common-among-black-women-and-more

Christy K, Kandasamy S, Majid U, Farrah K, Vanstone M. Understanding Black Women's Perspectives and Experiences of Cervical Cancer Screening: A Systematic Review and Qualitative Meta-synthesis. J Health Care Poor Underserved. 2021;32(4):1675-1697. doi: https://doi.org/10.1353/hpu.2021.0159 PMID: 34803036.

Coats, Thomas (2017). Clinical Importance of Treating Iron Overload in Sickle Cell Disease
https://clinicaltrials.gov/ct2/show/NCT00981370

Greger, Michael (2017). Plant vs. Animal Iron
https://nutritionfacts.org/2017/06/15/plant-versus-animal-iron/

American Heart Association (2021). What About African Americans and High Blood Pressure?
https://www.heart.org/-/media/Files/Health-Topics/Answers-by-Heart/What-About-African-Americans-and-HBP.pdf

Barnard, Neal (2006) Dr. Neal Barnard's Program for Preventing and Reversing Diabetes.

Hicklin, Tianna (2017) Factors Contributing to Higher Incidence of Diabetes in Black Americans.
https://www.nih.gov/news-events/nih-research-matters/factors-contributing-higher-incidence-diabetes-black-americans

Reynolds AN, Akerman AP, Mann J. Dietary fibre and whole grains in diabetes management: Systematic review and meta-analyses. PLoS Med. 2020 Mar 6;17(3):e1003053. doi: 10.1371/journal.pmed.1003053. PMID: 32142510; PMCID: PMC7059907.https://pubmed.ncbi.nlm.nih.gov/32142510/

CDC 2022. Fiber: The Carb That Helps You Fight Diabetes.
https://www.cdc.gov/diabetes/library/features/role-of-fiber.html

Esselstyn, Caldwell (2008). Prevent & Reverse Heart Disease.

BIBLIOGRAPHY

Barnard, Neal (2018). Power Foods for the Brain.

Brazier, Brendan (2017). Thrive.

Barnard, Neal (2020). Your Body in Balance.

Kaze, Arnaud D., Musani, Solomon K., Bidulescu, Aurelian, Correa, Adolfo, Bertoni, Alain G., Ahima, Rexford S., Golden, Sherita H., Abdalla, Marwah, Echouffo-Tcheugui, Justin B. (2021) Plasma Leptin and Blood Pressure Progression in Blacks, The Jackson Heart Study. Hypertension 2021; 77:1069-1075 https://www.ahajournals.org/doi/10.1161/HYPERTENSIONAHA.120.16174

Nicklas BJ, Toth MJ, Goldberg AP, Poehlman ET. Racial differences in plasma leptin concentrations in obese postmenopausal women. J Clin Endocrinol Metab. 1997 Jan;82(1):315-7. doi: 10.1210/jcem.82.1.3659. PMID: 8989280. https://pubmed.ncbi.nlm.nih.gov/8989280/

Jackson Heart Study: https://www.nhlbi.nih.gov/science/jackson-heart-study-jhs